The Bridge

The Bridge

by

Christopher Levenson

BuschekBooks

Canadian Cataloguing in Publication Data

Levenson, Christopher, 1934-
     The bridge

Poems.
ISBN 1-894543-02-5

     I. Title.

PS8573.E945B75 2000   C811'.54   C00-900973-6
PR9199.3.L464B75 2000

Printed in Winnipeg, Manitoba, Canada by Hignell Book Printing

The Canada Council | Le Conseil des Arts
for the Arts | du Canada

BuschekBooks gratefully acknowledges the support of the Canada Council for the Arts and the Ontario Arts Council for its publishing program.

BuschekBooks
P.O. Box 74053, 35 Beechwood Avenue, Ottawa, Ontario, Canada K1M 2H9
John Buschek, Editor

*For my grandson Aaron, my bridge into the twenty-first century,
and, as always, for Oonagh*

Table of Contents

Leavetaking

Activists

Mementoes

The Atlas

Leavetaking

Inspiration

A state of mind,
a New England state perhaps.
As I gaze from a markered freeway lookout
in a fold of hills and see miles of forest falling away
towards the distant ocean,
or chat with Fred the mechanic at the local garage
while my car's oil is changed,
and notice the streetlamps slowly coming on,
as though by inspiration, and dragging
the darkness like a barge behind them,
I am waiting for something to happen:
I tell myself
these are the turning points, not the grand moments—
the Liberation of Paris, the ballyhooed handshake
rehearsed between enemy statesmen, the photo op.

I never know
what's going to happen next. All I can do
is keep my wits about me and hope
when a big moment arrives
I will have words to hand, I will know what to do.

Leavetaking

My annual visit: I take you
in a rental car out of yourself,
confront you
for the first time in two years
with the sea. It is a painful progress
we make along the esplanade; you hang
on my arm, my words, as if
for dear life. You will have to store
the feel of winds over the cliffs,
the bluster of waves on the shingle,
for who knows how long now?
As I squire you through Lymington
we look at the swans, the ducks,
at a dockside inn take lunch,
I know all we have in common
is in the past, everywhere memories
scurry like granary mice.

Dad's death brought us back together
just as my brother's first
prised us apart, into silence,
but no words were left to assuage
fifteen years' absence, which cleaves us
like an unspoken reproach:
Even now I recall the dread,
my sometime truant mother,
of your unexplained departures,
long truces that never made way
for any enduring peace,
and then the divorce.
Through my whole adult life I tried
through a wilderness of women
to find solace for what was not said.
I failed, and my adolescence
was filled with marking your words
like the mottoes in fortune cookies,
how you 'can't abide waste', like a man
'to stand on his own two feet'.
You often reminded me

'If a thing's worth doing,
it's worth doing well.'

So what can I say? I lied,
told you of camping trips,
every Christmas sent Canadian
Wildlife Calendars,
but my news was sanitized:
no four letter-words, not a hint
one grandson perhaps was gay,
another maybe on drugs.
We developed rituals, to cross
an ocean of difference.

So, now you are gone for good,
what will I do with an eye
trained to clip animal photos
from newspapers, and hoard
foreign stamps that could somehow be sold
in Bournemouth for charity?
Outwardly dutiful,
whom shall I now phone on Sundays?
The rhododendrons' purple
candelabra that lit up
your willed seclusion here
in a second more lush suburbia
I shall not disturb again.
Now with your ashes scattered
over the rose garden,
inland, away from the sea,
we seem to have made
too late an uneasy peace.

Bonfire

The room divests itself
of warmth, of furniture,
delivers up its ghost;
even the fake-electric
coal-fire goes out,
disconnected
along with your life-support
of neighbours and distant friends,
whose steady drift of postcards
from ten, twenty years back,
are silenced witnesses to all
who held you dear.

I, hasty executor,
hold court over these remains,
having neither time nor space
to take anything back,
except for a few books,
a clutch of photographs,
not even a single word.
As for bedlinen, curtains,
when I ask around it seems nothing
is wanted any more,
all values personal.

Late October: driving back
after the service, I watch
men burning leaves on a bonfire.
My eyes smart, blur with the smoke
that scrawls upon my brow
the ashes of memory.

Old Mothers

Mothers live on
too little, uncomplaining or, at least,
discreet in their dissatisfaction, insist
they can get by

on one phone call
a month, a Christmas letter, 'no flowers
thank you'. They scuttle like hermit crabs out to
local stores and

back, otherwise
hide behind screens of photographs and lace,
awaiting visits, passing the time of day,
afraid of flu

and falling down
in public places, compromising their
hard-won independence. Used now to going
to funerals

of friends, they too
have chosen their plots, they have developed
character and intend to see it through till
the curtain falls.

The Tool Shed

for my father

Beyond the kitchen door,
ramshackle, it hoarded
not just rakes and garden hose,
twine, fertilizer, bulbs,
a rusted tricycle,
but also dust-festooned
trophies of your life
before I was born, a past
abandoned to marriage:
your time in Nigeria as
Lord Leverhulme's interpreter.
This you rarely spoke of,
showed me few photographs,
but l recall unlatching,
past woodlouse and centipede,
almost a shrine long sealed
in jungled memories:
native drums, a one string fiddle,
carved ebony figurines.
One summer while I was off
in Europe or Canada
you donated them all to some
deserving charity.

Instead at every free moment
you bent your mind and back
over rock garden succulents,
on which you heaped such tender,
composted love. Under your hands
overblown dahlias grew,
chrysanthemums, hollyhocks,
for every mild season some
new blooms to wonder at.
In peace time no longer
'digging for victory',
you supplied the dinner table
with tomatoes, runner beans, chives
and made us seem self-sufficient
while on each window sill

fierce cacti stood on guard.
The only thing that failed
was a peach tree sprung from a stone
that hung over our neighbour's yard.
At my mother's urging you moved it
to the middle of the lawn
where it shrivelled and died.
Now whatever I know
of the names of plants, of patience,
I have from you.

But I never put on
either your interest or skill,
a window box my limit.
The tools you left were dispersed,
sold with the house, I suppose.
A few years back I walked past.
The front lawn had been paved
and the tool shed torn down:
now it's a two car garage.
The renovators did
such a skilful cover up
no archeologist could
unearth what used to be.

Esperanto

for my father

For you it was
a shorthand for hope, never mastered,
the grammars undusted among
the faded orange soft covers
of the Left Book Club
when castles in Fascist Spain
were abandoned for communes in Russia
and The Future was possible.

I am glad you did not survive
to witness the New World Order
with its 'thousand points of light'
proclaiming Babel through
the Pentecostal tongues
of Baghdad and Sarajevo,
nations united in fire.
Our words have been dispossessed
by tracer flares, mortar shells;
privatising our griefs,
we are left with smatterings.

For My Brother, Fifty Years Dead

It took forever, that trip,
one nondescript Saturday:
first the Tube, then the North London line:
at eleven for me it was all
uncharted territory.
Then this graveyard in Isleworth:
why would they put you there,
so far away from home?
I have never been back

My first death was a grief
I had no words for then
but have since grown into,
and carry under my heart
like an inoperable
tumour. Often since
I have tried to imagine how
as adults we might have met,
come together, or parted
in anger, and every March
your death sinks in like snow.

Geode

On the edge of everything, fifty minutes out
from Charing Cross by Underground, Canons Park,
still not the countryside, a random nothingness:
these trim privet hedges, prize dahlias, crazy paving,
imposed a routine of silence. Our unknown neighbours
stifled behind lace curtains and garden gnomes.

My teenage years were a waiting, a lying in wait
for a life to begin, somewhere different. Cambridge?
In any case, away. Meanwhile, inside
my mother moved out of the matrimonial bed,
folded herself into my dead brother's room.
My father and I said nothing, semi-detached.

So for years strata of feeling, makeshift solitudes,
were compressed into acquiescence. But like a geode
I felt my unshed tears slowly harden to crystal.
The youth I had lost took three deaths to emerge
as simple stone resolved into amethyst,
a code of absence, secret until broken.

Luxuries

Growing up
on the puritan pungencies
of Wrights Coal Tar Soap and Dettol—
no car, no telephone, or central heating—
but plenty of milk, fresh air,
long hikes in the Pennines,
I find now when I see
those limousines sidle past, sleek
plush-padded cells of privacy,
or glimpse from afar
posh executive suites replete
with every kind of turn-on,
I am not envious. How much
can a single person take?
How many cars are enough?
private jets? yachts? jacuzzis?
How many acres of broadloom?

I used to live near Canons,
the model for Timon's Villa,
now an exclusive girls' school,
but nothing rubbed off:
my father as he pottered in the toolshed
hummed the Internationale. My tiny family
was big on brotherhood—
the Co-op Women's Guild, the striking miners.
We were undemonstrative misfits
in our North London suburb,
Quaker revolutionaries.

Like Baker Mountain hanging above the horizon,
it is still a long way off,
that dream of equality,
'to each according to his need',
four walls, firewood, a roof,
a lake of clear water,
a few thousand feet of clean air.

Preludes-1

Always the possible
                 saltflats expanding
                                 beyond the horizon:

plateaus
                  palisades
                                 of cloudspace

framing the sun,
                  shot skies
                                 towards evening

above the estuary
                  the water opaque
                                 opal-resilient.

It is to this
                  I return
                                 thinking of childhood,

this and the distant
                  Lake District mountains
                                 (merely hills

in any but a child's
                  word-chest)
                                 and Druce Farm

with its five grey cats
                  and the pet sheep
                                 and the shore

and the wide bay beyond
                  and further still

                                 the possible ocean.

Preludes-2

A gurgling baby voice
          under gorse, turf, heather
                    the beck
whose banks we walked beside
          Mum, Dad, Geoffrey and I
                    on our frequent
weekend excursions
          to Clougha
                    a whale-grey fell
barely a mountain
          that we could make out
                    a few miles off
from our bedroom windows
          a permanence
                    a flank of the Pennines.
Once we got beyond
          a certain stile
                    stepping stones
there was no going back
          only the bleat
                    of bewildered sheep,
the sudden skyward lurch
          of a curlew
                    from its nest in long grass,
a few arthritic trees
          the wind bent double
                    a silence broken
only by our steps
          or rain squalls
                    no hope of shelter
nothing but a few cairns
          a coldharbour
                    lichened rocks
not even when we got there
          much of a view
                    but I felt taken in,
at home in this countryside:
          force, beck, ghyll
                    I know

I have a right

to these words

I grew up with them

they sluice my inner ear

remain like the stream

a distant lullaby,

constant accompaniment

of misted limestone hills

I need them still

to make my peace.

Preludes-3

Why in my memory
                          was it always
                                                      raining,
those weekends we visited
                          Ingleton, hill town
                                                      on the west slopes of the Pennines?
After picnicking
                          by the caves, the waterfalls
                                                      these were my first
oilskinned intrusions
                          underground:
                                                      past stalagmites, stalagtites—
the pre-war guide book found
                          fanciful names for all their
                                                      dripping shapes—
like miners
                          we huddled, groped through
                                                      torrential war-time dark
back towards light.
                          Nothing spectacular,
                                                      yet I enjoyed
the damp bracken,
                          fish and chips at the Tea Rooms
                                                      before the bus ride home
clutching against my chest
                          an atmosphere
                                                      of stone walls, of enduring.

Preludes-4

At the butt-end
          of war-time Morecambe
                    abandoned beyond
the blacked-out holiday palaces
          lampless piers
                    grand boarded-up hotels
Heysham Head
          with its tiny zoo
                    shabby hand-me-down brown bear
offered flat rocks
          by the shore
                    where we spread out
our Sunday picnic salad,
          home-made cheese flan
                    and I ran like a seagull,
flapping my arms
          and screaming
                    at my first extended
taste of the sea,
          a vision of distances
                    in the miniature
landscapes of rockpools
          crab, seaweed, shells
                    all we could handle then
as evacuees
          yet this has proved
                    a more enduring home to me
than Edgware, that shifty
          North London suburb,
                    the Norman church
of simple ancient stone
          the cottage that sold
                    nettle wine
though my parents fobbed me off
          with ginger beer
                    still in stone bottles then
and grey horizons
          as far as Ireland
                    over a hostile sea.

Preludes-5

This was a routine

I never tired of,

the afternoon bus

beyond Carnforth

then Warton

a huddle of farms

only two hundred feet

above sea level

but so remote

in July or August sun

as we struck out

for the crags

and blackberries

scrambling over

fissures, rock faces

for the dangling prizes

landing in nettles

filling

our ears with sea-wind and bird cry

grazing our arms

on barbed-wire brambles

Slowly we filled

the steel milk canisters

high with a fragrant blackness,

half of what we had gathered

the rest had been

internalized, ripeness

tested on the tongue

over and over like a new word

until, stigmata

on bared arms and legs,

we sweated back to the bus

with stained, purple mouths.

Ex-wife

In the rainshadow of divorce
we dry up, hardly a word falls all year
except when our children, go-betweens, explore
the arid river-beds, provoke unwittingly
sometimes a flash-flood
of anger or remorse to plunder the gulch;
otherwise nothing.

Yet in new, separate lives
at times we still steal a glance
at their lost inheritance, reckon up secretly
those frozen assets of memories
we cannot redistribute or transfer,
interests we had and can no longer share.

Inter-city 125

In late October this has become a new country for me:
speed has transformed its elegaic green almost beyond
recognition, it is my own no more.
Childhood is packed away like Christmas decorations or medals,
only for special occasions. I watch in disbelief a stagnant countryside
archaic now, the land crawls with abandoned nissen huts,
warehouses, crumbling brick, bright red Victorian hospitals
a chaos of viaducts, gantries and on canals monkey boats:
in wartime they hauled coal now gaudy, like floating gipsy caravans,
leisure craft merely. Then suddenly set amid trees
this foursquare manor house of Cotswold stone, distinctive
among the chicken factories' council estates' routine, anonymous neatness.

Gradually after Preston the North takes hold, hedges subside
into stone walls. In their own right for all their small scale,
mountains impose on us granite, whitewashed barns, lashed woods
straddling the ridge, homogeneities of grey but homely, welcoming.
The rain infringes on moorlands, sheep combed by the wind,
rough crags carding the clouds sunlight trawling a distant fell.
Still we run on, unheeding. Below me in meadows deer graze, hardly look up,
a synod of pheasants whirrs into flight from heather.
But too one-sided, this sliding past at 80 framed in aero-dynamic
brushed steel: until I can get down among the brawl
of becks, cowsheds, walk the damp-shawled woods, I must make do,
make believe I am coming home, I cannot reclaim.

29

On Rediscovering An Iowa City Address Book

They're mostly babysitters, hosts of them, composite,
ex-students, with that well-built, healthy look,
farm-fresh, German or Scandinavian stock.
They did not join in our demos.
But well-known names too: Vance Bourjaily
('The man who knew Kennedy') at whose farm in Fall '67
attending a pig-roast to raise campaign funds
for Eugene McCarthy,
our eyes grew smoky with hope and alcohol.
Kurt Vonnegut too, for a while, and Nelson Algren
('The man with the golden arm') and dozens of writers
like Borges, Guillevic, Berryman, just passing through
'the Athens of the Mid-West'. We brushed against
their greatness in a dark bar
and wore the encounter like a wound for months.

Others maybe have flourished elsewhere, beyond earshot:
the sculptor, Malcolm Gimse, whose maquette of Lazarus
still rises over my chest of drawers,
and grad. student friends now dispersed across the States
or the world. Where is Brigitte Mach,
tall, red-haired, extravagant German?
or Leroy and Yvonne? It was in their Quonset hut
I first heard the Kingston Trio playing 'Love is blue'.
Love turned out a blue baby for them all right:
she took the kids back to Mormon Idaho, he, newly mated,
went on to a Doctorate.

But there's some I'd rather forget, like the critic and writer
who drunkenly told my Director of Studies, his host,
and a holocaust survivor, 'next time we'll make sure no one ecapes.'

For sure, no one escapes:
we have all grown greyer, plumper, more complacent,
wear political correctness like a bullet-proof vest.
But nothing can bring back
the real fever of knowing what was right
and what was good for a world that seemed so simple.

The black vinyl cover closes over them.
I stow the book. We have been disconnected.
There is no service for the numbers I have dialed,
the past remains opaque.

In The Rough

I
Burnt out from decades flying world-wide
business class, he is afraid of airports,
hardly dares set foot in one to greet
his favourite sister, visiting
after years abroad, bringing the gift of pain.
Before it had been the ocean, always there
since childhood, his one horizon. It was
the family trade and he, fresh out of school,
spent ten years in the merchant navy, sailing the world,
returned laden with a seething hold of memories.

II
More at ease on the golf course nowadays,
he ponders what force to apply
to a five foot putt, in the club house later
replays his game with cronies. At home with a pint
and half an eye on T.V., the Irish 0pen, his mind
like a cow's stomach regurgitates
every swing, every stroke. To his teenage nephew,
a skilful acolyte, he repeats: 'Keep your head down!'
Grouse-like, he blends into his chosen landscape
away from all turbulence; this immaculate green
is beyond reproach, a veneer of the civilized..
Enforced retirement has not come easily,
his days still busy, planning
how to forget.

III
Uneasy the pride he takes in his father's medals,
press cuttings from the *Irish Times*, the immaculate
public persona displayed behind glass:
haphazard affairs, the drinking, the absence, 'the mother' left
to fend as best she could. He keeps his head down, will not view
the carefully preserved corpse of his own childhood
buried at sea, then disgorged onto the strand.

IV
Wave upon wave the sea washes over him,
the sea that fashioned him he will not hear
crashing his memory. For now it seems enough
to concentrate on handling the chipper, lofting the ball
out of the long grass into the fairway.
He thinks there is still time. On the headland over the town
he chooses his iron, appraises distances;
the coast is clear, no voices reach out to him.

Mountain Climbing

for Oonagh

'Marrying you', your friend said, 'would be like
climbing a mountain.'   I certainly didn't have
the right boots, had not been in training;
and yet there was, is still, an exhilaration
in the expense of energy, a reward in the view
over several sunlit counties, an achievement, glory even,
in the expanse of air, the effort, the sudden
clumps of wildflowers springing from rock-faces,
the rise and fall of the pathways, the need to press on.
We made it, after three hours reached the summit.

But at a mere three thousand feet this is enough:
I've no ambition
to tackle the Andes or the Himalayas.

The Compass

for Oonagh

This instrument becomes you:
its quivering needle
is sensitive to the earth's pull
as you are, all senses alert
to my heavy, lumbering tread
or clumsy, well-meaning words.
So, confident in tact,
you can strike out a path between
gorse bushes, heather, screes,
and take your bearings before
the last hard climb or detour.
And if it makes you more
at home in the world, at ease,
for me that is enough.
Take it as talisman, guide
to help you find your way
finally through dark woods
into the free air.

Activists

Fireflies

Bosnia, 1961

At dusk in the low hills above Bihac
all I can make out of the town
is random light from cottages,
arc-lamps by the marshalling yards
and at the station sparks from the waiting loco
adrift with steam.
But all around me in the humid night
thousands of fireflies hover and disappear
like memories, foreboding ash.

Peacekeeping

As I turn from the TV News
in multicultural Canada
and shots of our Blue Berets
dispensing aid and comfort,
a few words of Serbo-Croat
percolate through
my thirty years absence.
I tell them like worry beads,
the places I visited,
Banja Luka, Bihac, Mostar
all after fifty years
again strategic in
the war against refugees.
Mnogo sam zaboravao:
'1 have forgotten much'
that now comes back to me
with a bitter aftertaste.

How can I keep my peace?
Memories there outlast
families, empires.
Children suckle on
a mediaeval hatred
quick as a shot to dispute
each acre of barren rock.
Though I loved the land I saw
in its entirety,
I must have ignored the ghosts.
Now everywhere desperate knuckles
of schist thrust out of the ground:
every massacre
will some day exact its due,
blood for familiar blood,
hacked bone for bone.

How then can I be freed
from the treason of memory?
What way to reconcile
how at a dairy bar

in Sarajevo I bought
cottage cheese freshly wrapped
in a large leaf,
or laughed as I heard four horsemen
reeking of slivovica
sing as they spurred uphill
into the waiting dusk?
Does it matter that I watched
kerchiefed women dancing the kolo
on the station platform, or gazed
down alleyways flagged with washing
to the harbour at Korchula?
No words can console,
there is no peace to rest in.

The Bridge

for Tahsin and Gülser

Why had I thought them secure,
these memories? The walls
of ancient fortresses, sails crowding the quays,
a market square
where water melons were stacked like cannon balls?
Even the bridge at Mostar
that lasted five hundred years, a masterpiece,
is history. At home we shuffle
through folk dance tapes, photographs:
nothing can restore
the lost cities. Always what is built
later on vacant sites superimposes, throws
the mind off its scent. True, it is only stone,
carved wood, bone ornaments,
and their peasant custodians
have been driven out or killed,
even ancestral cemeteries destroyed,
but though earthquake or flood
do the same work, transforming
a once familiar landscape, in time
we can accept that cost far easier
than the same damage done by a neighbour's hand:
these buildings, castle and mosque, are what
helped them survive, part of what shaped them into
Serb, Croat, Bosnian, gave them
continuity. Now when so much is gone
that made us human all the world over, where
do we find the heart to begin again?

Gods

1.

From my nineteenth floor office I watch
strung out in gaudy snow suits
the daycare children's chain gang
shout past the library.
In labs through two-way mirrors
their games are observed, their body language
studied and filed away.
When they become adult
they will be silenced.

2.

On a TV special the bitterness of womanflesh
sages femmes, midwives, branded
for untimely wisdom, a way with herbs,
are thrown to the flames, for skills
they could not keep to themselves.

3.

Twenty-four hours after the operation
my four month old Bouvier pup
totters stupefied to her food.
I have decided for her,
I do not want her to breed.
Grateful, she licks my hand,
dozes most of the day.
She is better adapted now,
will return to her old, young self
relieved of sexuality,
to concentrate on food,
human affection.

4.

One August out of a blue sky
roofers working next door thought they'd destroy
a wasps' nest slung from a branch on a front lawn tree
and with a blow-lamp set light
to the intricately wrought grey paper metropolis.
Its spirals unfurled as the flames caught
and the dazed wasps fumed out, spun burning, or fell to the grass.
Slow ash floated down and all that was left
was a brown smudge on the branch, a few shrivelled leaves.

5.

It's like a relay race:
a man of many parts, I sign away
my liver, kidneys, heart;
my driver's license bequeathes
to the hospital's body shop
whatever's in good repair.
I know there is always someone
with needles and pumps sustaining
the bare presence of life, those white
lies of existence, lying in wait
for me to die, for a
specialist to decide
who has the best case.
As long as there are victims
the steely Cyclops eye
at the operating table
cannot be put out.

6.

The Goddess moves with the slow river, the fields,
empowering harvest. The earth does not resist
rockfalls, volcanoes, it has known it all before—
Krakatoa, St Helens—all in its own good time
the lava will settle down, plants will eventually grow
overcoming the wilderness, take root
between the barren stones. Just give the garden time.

Canberra

Homage to geometry:
to measure up against the earth
the natural skyline of gum trees,
earth tones, a map of the future
blueprinted onto an otherwise undistinguished
tract of bush, since the 1830s
a few parcels of land, no settlement,
no roads, only dusty tracks between hills
where now a triangle
of broad avenues, an artificial
lake, vistas of white marble
converge on parliament. These breathtaking
lurches of steel, soaring glass, the outlines
of office blocks, art gallery, high court
beside the water, stir me despite myself,
seeing the plan enacted after fifty years, a city
almost complete, running like clockwork, clean,
along its pre-ordained axes,
the span of every bridge
a masterpiece, each angle
gracefully calculated.

It is the kind of thing
I had always wanted,
for Britain, for Canada,
a model community:
for pedestrians and motorists
there is a place, for small children to play
a place, for hospitals, gardens, a place
for concert halls, museums, national libraries,
but no unruly growth, no ground
where the weed imagination can take root, no space
between these tidy paving stones and hydrants
for brush to grow
unnoticed in back lots.

I wander the streets and miss
ramshackle corner stores,
contraptions of rusted iron,
the scrawl of barbed wire by oil drums,
benched old men haunting the public parks
and the young mothers
talking by crumbling gateposts while their kids
cry havoc, and everywhere the smudge,
the smear, the lichen of human prints,
the makeshift splendour
of tumbleweed over desert roads, the accident
drifting within us, evidence
that outlives any machine.

Occasions

The Taj Mahal at dawn: busloads wait every day
for this 'very unique' experience.
In the High Andes and the Himalayas
maybe there are still places not yet pre-packaged.
Even the candlelight dinner
at our weekend hideaway in the Kawarthas
had its cover blown Saturday in the *Globe and Mail*.

The travel agents have sized us up, got us covered,
shrink-wrapped for risk-free safaris.
They arrange for the rain-forest waterfall to be turned on
as the tourist train reels past. The four-star romantic views
have all been foreseen and every camera angle
accounted for: back at the cruise ship
plastic souvenirs 'made in Hong Kong' are stacked and waiting.

Likewise the year's highlights. Christmas and Easter
flash by like suburban stations. Fairs and festivals
put a happy face on Sunday's tense boredom.
Coronations and State Weddings 'made for TV'
leave us unsatisfied. Six months later on the wedding cake
after the mice have nibbled away inside
only the icing remains.

With everything on view twenty-four hours a day,
like squirrels we hoard our silences, preserve
secret corners of marriages and deaths
unrecorded, for us alone, and let
occasions come on us suddenly, unprepared,
without polaroid or fixed smile. We ad lib happiness,
hope it will do for now.

Activists

For more than thirty years in unison
we have been 'overcoming'
in marches and candle-light vigils, protest rallies.
Now once again, rag-tag Utopians, we gather
in a downtown park, overlooked by high-rise condos,
overlooked by the media or good at most
for a ten second sound bite.
Grey-haired, solid citizens, what has come over us
that we are still the same
Quakers and Unitarians, trade unionists, social workers
arrested and jailed in the sixties for demanding an end
to the Missile Crisis, the Vietnam War,
for mourning slain civil rights workers, arranging sit-ins
in college presidents' offices, proclaiming
a woman's right to choose?
Somehow we did not pass on
the torch of discontent, the belief in action.
We still picket for an end to low-level flights
over Innu land, or to lance our outrage
when a woman is forced to return to Jamaica
to a husband who'd sworn to kill her.

One of my students tells me
hers is a generation of bystanders.
I pray it may not be so, knowing how much
prayers have achieved in my lifetime:
screams prevail where banners will not. In the end
the numbers count: half a million meet
by the Lincoln Memorial and they will be heard;
a single, high-profile martyr
outweighs a hundred committees. I know too
that as long as the palms of the powerful
have to be greased with blood
we must still stand up, however few, to be counted.

Mementoes

Grand Trunk Canal

for David Craig

Already setting out into the half-light
for an after-dinner walk seems to take on
a further meaning. Feeling our way
along a tow-path overgrown with sedge,
conspiracies of wind and leaf decoy me
through sheltering willow and alder
once more into my war childhood.

All I see is changed:
untended hedgerows, obsolete coppices,
green water latched with weeds, the silent light
of the cottage by the broken lock-gate. No one about.
Though I sigh and turn back, my mind adrift, returns.

Often I'd come here with the family.
There is no way
to restore those week-end rambles, summer picnics
in the long grass beside the canal to Carnforth,
but smells persist—the reek of railway ties
soaked in fresh creosote where the boats unloaded
at Glasson Dock—and the place my father showed me
my first kingfisher flashing through the reeds
or I gazed in envy at the monkey boats,
crews unperturbed,
chugging through troubled countryside, self-contained
and into green oblivion. Although unspoken,
sharing this with you makes a communion,
something to shore against
times when we cannot move so easily, or be moved.

Still Life On The Scottish Border, 1952

Under the fir trees or in the fire rides, spades,
mattocks, are stacked like rifles, crude cement pipes
surround a bothie where at lunch break the men sprawl
with open bait tins for 'a wee bit crack' and a smoke.
No words strike fire from the circle of stone faces.
The ganger swigs tea from a chipped metal mug.
And with no tall tales of past wars, the conchies wait
in macs and wellingtons, afraid to read
in case *Ulysses, Crime and Punishment* provoke their scorn.
The bulldozer and the dump trucks reek of hot oil.
Stones and mud accumulate, the hills brood, the rain does not let up.

Birdwatching

in memoriam Judy Kennedy

The cliffs at Filey, 1953:
after the giddy heights of love we fall
on grass. I lie still, you gaze over the edge
at 'crows and choughs that wing the midway air',
and redshanks, black-headed gulls, sandpipers far below.
I am bored, maybe jealous, seeing your attention
so soon diverted, shared with birds.

It took me years to recognize their beauty:
a decade later a Wisconsin friend drove me along
the Mississippi to glimpse bald eagles in their eyries;
my first April in Ottawa from the rooftop restaurant
of the Skyline Hotel I heard the long honking V
of Canada Geese returning three hundred feet up,
and was stirred; my first evening in New Delhi
green parakeets shuttled the dusk; in Canberra
crimson and indigo parrots transformed suburban shrubs
to circuses. Gradually over the years
birds flew free from the tapestry of landscape
and nested in my mind.

A long fuse it was you lit that day in Filey.
We went our separate ways, oceans apart, wrote seldom,
and only now do I know what you did for me then:
love opens our eyes to the world beyond,
to the world within. I see,
I see.

The New House

Cosier, easy to keep clean,
air-conditioned throughout, central vac.:
the Realtor, Mariette,
was ecstatic on our behalf.
Unconcerned now about schools,
after only twenty minutes we took it,
mainly for the view of the river.

Now we are settled in we find
there is no basement for the unexpected
leftovers of our children, or for magazines
that are sure to come in handy once they're gone.
There is still too much in storage.

But for the time being
I am consoled each dawn
by the song of the phoebe, by watching
beavers swim, now in now under
the water to their lodge
and its secret entrances.

A Century

for Sidney Fooks, on his 100th birthday

1.

Near Ithaca, New York, arriving at a friend's farmhouse
before him, Oonagh and I were invited in
to the cool, low-beamed kitchen, introduced
to Jim's mother, past ninety, silver-haired, skin translucent
like her hare-bell eyes, but a bird-like brightness
gleaming through between spells of dozing.
At the other end of the room a day-old kid,
brought in from the goat-pen outside, by its mother abandoned,
lay curled and whitely bleating in a wicker basket
beside the hearth: these two at opposite ends
performed their delicate balancing act of life and frailty.
And now with my grandson's four kittens, a huddle of ginger, calico, tabby,
only five days old, still blind, I am amazed
how anything lives beyond childhood.

2.

But somehow they do survive: my good friend, Anthony
saw his son Oliver's early talent for cricket, told me how
a few years back, on impulse he had flown
from Bristol to Sri Lanka, half way round the world,
to watch him bat for the M.C.C. Junior Eleven
greeting him only later, unannounced, in his son's hotel lobby.
I did not see that match, can only imagine
the careful placing of strokes, the drives through cover,
the defensive blocks, the confident boundaries,
as he slowly built from fifty to a hundred,
with all the players applauding when he walked back
to the pavilion. Yes, there is luck but also
style and resourcefulness, resilient strength.

3.

So Sidney, you also
amassed your century: after a full career,
in retirement you stuck with what you knew best, painting, and poetry,
gardening, memories,

outliving two wives and making your peace
with what could not now be changed—the thought of those you had seen
slain on the Somme and at Passchendaele, all that bewilderment
of wasted life—and taking in gratitude
unlooked for yet accepted, the extra years,
though almost blind now still reading, listening to tapes,
and somehow still writing letters in a firm hand.
Confined to your Gloucestershire hills, set back from the road
but seemingly content with what is left you,
you earn our standing applause, and I who had thought myself
one of a tiny band of loyal ex-pupils,
find there are thirty two who still keep in touch
'forty years on' with their old English master, a tribute
that tells you something of how your life was spent.
Like carrier pigeons our thoughts
circle and land, and we are with you now.

A Moveable Homeland

for Adela and Guillermo,
on their Golden Wedding Anniversary

To have survived so long together argues
a kind of grace, a golden mean, a meaning
beyond dates in passports, the expired visas
that mark your wanderings, We only see
its outward signs, the visible content,
how you acclimatize to age and how from exile
you have drawn strength, a sense of hard-won
achievement, preserving in each other
a moveable homeland

Though, God knows, you have been whittled enough
by deaths, by distances,
what has remained is clarity,
a matching vigour living to the full
however long you are given, and it is good to see
how from all the arguments like volcanic ash
the soil grows more fertile, the walls resilient enough
to withstand earthquakes. So the scientist's calm inquiry
combines with the musician's sense of time,
exacting its own harmony, like the view
of Mount Aconcagua always on the horizon
as you drove back to the ocean. May it stay with you,
crowding the sunset with pacific gold.

Prospect

For D.G.J.

From his director's chair on the half-finished deck,
Doug views the first rushes of the valley—
spruce, tamarack and maple. Somewhere a stream
tests its sole woodwind against the green orchestra
and in the invisible distance beyond woods
a truck growls uphill. The haze is riddled with birdsong.
This summer another two months of work, perhaps
some day a pool, a garden. For now at least
the doors and windows are set, the roof shingled,
walls and floors fragrant with cedar. From sheer imagining
on a Quebec hillside the patient artificer
has erected a new space. He sees that it is good.

The Voice

for Ruth Martin

I knew only your voice,
imperious, demanding,
over the telephone.

No nonsense here, I thought.
You'd set the facts down so,
wait for an answer.

Though you grew sick,
that voice stayed firm till near the end,
kept your life on an even keel.

Now you are gone I miss
the scanty words we shared:
your voice will not let go.

A Poem For Enid

Often I think of you, Enid, passionate, writing like crazy—
of politics, family, people you loved or admired—
as you whittled away at what little was left of a childhood
in Flin Flon, your Winnipeg medical studies
aborted by early motherhood. You endured marriage, divorce.

True, in the poetry group you were sometimes a pain, but I miss
your drunken, gusty laughter as, swaddled in smoke,
your mind still keen like a Loblaws plastic bag
crammed with compassion and rags and defiant hope,
you swayed between beer and bouts of poetry.

Yes, you were weak, as all of us sometimes are
in our different ways, but you never gave up
on yourself or on others and were absurdly grateful
for small, remembered mercies, you who were prodigal
with love and enthusiasm. You were one tough lady,

and never deserved such a messy death, a reproach to us all
in the treed and fully-serviced lots of our poetry.
You found your peace in the local Anglican church,
in your friends and your cats. Now God has got to you.

How much will survive? Who knows? Who ever knows?
But at least you were not marginal; you were the real thing.

Archipelagoes

for Don and Heidi

At most once a year we visit,
have dinner together, talk well
into the night, so that in memory
our words reverberate in this space
we set aside and hold up to our gaze
like a monstrance, an island
reliably there still
on the horizon.

Over the years, approaching
by boat from the mainland of our
daily lives, we can with binoculars
make out a rock face, a familiar
stand of trees,
each island different, and still
below the surface deduce
the unseen mountain range that confers purpose,
emerging now and then into these peaks,
an archipelago.

Cirque Du Soleil

It is about the body,
                         fluent limbs soaring
buoyed beyond words, beyond...

It is about perilous shifts,
                         the sudden turning
choreographed for wrist and ankle,
                         bonding with ropes
sixty feet up, the trapeze, the high
                         wire strung out across
our tautened nerves in the dark
                         tent overshadowed by
fanfares of colour, pulsating
                         cascades of music.
It is about lithe figures' enthralling
                         slow spotlit progress
towards ultimate risk, muscled intensities.

Who has not yearned for solo flight, for wings,
                         for the impossible
learnt inarticulate balance and
                         timing, the letting go
onto the dark arena of all our senses—
                         that streamlined swoop
and last-second recovery,
                         poise, control, release
above the applauding crowds?
                         It is about body
becoming spirit, transcending.

Mementoes

for Peter Dale Scott

Skopje, Verona, Lancaster, Les Baux:
in your poem I come across references
to places I lived in or long since visited,
and begin to understand how,
like those fishermen forever mending their nets
on the quays at Portofino, each of us weaves
a purse skein from a million strands of nerve endings
to catch the shoals of our past: knotting together
impressions so they will hold
is all the proof we need that we have existed.
In this web silver flickers of photograph, a smile
from a passing face, a postcard
addressed and stamped but unsent,
are points of contact that flare
like shot silk as we move evanescent
slowly into darkness. This is the world
I have woven out of my time,
this is what I remember,
the air in the monastery precinct quivering still
after the angelus,
first light on distant mountains.

The Atlas

The Atlas

In war-time doing my childish bit for the Allies
with my Aircraft Spotters guide,
I could tell from their black silhouettes
what had hit us, Heinkel or Messerschmidt.
Each evening after the six o'clock news I would watch
my father between stints as an Air Raid Warden
pencil into the Atlas
Uncle Joe Stalin's advances
or, after the Second Front, ours.
Names of rivers, Vistula, Don
cities like Rostock, Benghazi,
the shape of the Normandy coastline—
a thousand unnatural landscapes
were imprinted on memory.

But years before that,
thanks to my 'Uncle' Hellmuth
(who reluctantly went back to Hamburg in '39
to do *his* bit) or maybe, Mr. Schlesinger
(a German Jew, who'd left us his books for safe keeping
when he was interned as an 'enemy alien')
I had gorged on full page photographs
*Im Fluge durch die Welt**, a coffee table book
from before the Great War and gazed in awe at
Buenos Aires, Sydney, Yellowstone, Hong Kong, Dresden—
whose fires I could not blow out on my eleventh birthday.
Somehow when my father died the book was mislaid or sold:
now I can never explain why I had to see
with my own eyes as much as there was time for,
how I had to take on the world.

*In Flight through the World

Travel Agency

My first doodlings were maps
of amoeba-like fantasy islands,
based on 'Swallows and Amazons',
but urban: pirate treasure
gave way to railroads, bridges,
imagined cities' street plans.
I even devised time tables
for phantom bus companies.

Then, teenage suburban prospector,
I sauntered around Mayfair,
Charing Cross, into the City,
stopped in at shipping offices
to pick up cruise brochures,
dallying with the air
of a world traveller.

And once or twice mum and dad
made use of my services
to plan a holiday,
but mostly the maps and pamphlets
that littered my bedroom shelves
—glossy *Arizona Highways*,
'Fall in Connecticut'—
only nurtured my dreams.

Now I have been right round
the world, but I am still
not satisfied: This rage for fantasy
seduces me into drafting
plateau and river mouth.
The amoebas proliferate, places
take on a life of their own,
invade my memory.

Frontiers

Bodyguards everywhere are paid not to be themselves
but to represent—
'Order', 'Security' - and only when
we have passed beyond earshot or gunshot
do we look around and see how subtly the world
has changed for us, not merely language or landscape
and product names on the billboards,
but the way stooks are tied, cottages colour-washed,
kinds of food, shapes of faces.
So much now is international and agreed, so many flavours
homogenized, one wonders at times why travel
when it is all a yard away on TV.

A few clean breaks remain: once, entering
Slovenia by train through a tunnel,
the new country came with the dynamite blasting of light
after darkness, enclosure.
Flying removes the problem: we are there without warning;
with no time to prepare a face, strangeness is forced upon us.
But mostly, on land, we slowly become aware
of a different rhythm, familiar gestures that here
have other meanings,
new ways of smiling, more impulsive speech, and are grateful
to get outside ourselves, to try on for size
a fresh identity.

So with marriage, bereavement, ageing, our own deaths,
we enter by a slow acclimatization,
observing the lie of the land, picking up clues from the natives
until, fully at home in the new state of mind, of heart,
we find ourselves in turn directing strangers.

New Delhi Street Theatre

for Aloke and Aunjona

An updated Mystery Cycle, they come in a mini-bus
to the back entrance of the Presidential Palace,
this tiny troupe Aloke had scoured from the streets, as is,
and trained. In seconds they are ready,
with sound system and lights festooned from the trees,
and start to the beat of a single drum,
tumblers and acrobats, dancers and clown, performing
to a sprawl of laughing children of chauffeurs, gardeners,
in a shaded yard far from official India.

In white-face, speaking Hindi, they assume
in turn the urgent masks
of crack dealer, junkie, landlord.
Now a bridegroom's family holds out for a larger dowry.
They strut, threaten, entreat, collapse in pain.
The children, squatting, look on,
their bright circle of faces, puzzled, amused,
but for me, also in white-face,
the body language translates easily
into dangerous truths. On edge behind washing lines,
the mothers stand in doorways, unsure what it is
their children are absorbing. Is this disloyalty
they are too young to handle, will these scenes outsmart, or lead to,
communal violence? The children are caught up
in the drama of their own lives, today, tomorrow.

The tableau ends suddenly, props disassembled, stowed.
Like units in a guerrilla war, the actors depart, melt back
into the urban forest, no victory certain.

Long Distance

for Gieve

At all hours I try to call you, to
restore contact. Under the ringing tone,
porous, a mesh of voices
in tongues I cannot make out—Marathi? Gujurati?
in a city I have twice visited. How in this Babel
will I get through?

Who knows what's happening there? News clips
don't tell it all. Maybe,
since you last wrote, private disasters.
I calculate, half a world away,
ten and a half time zones, how you will be
asleep or, already in your tomorrow,
leaving for work, relaxing after a meal.

I hoped I had found a friend
for the long haul. Tell me it is so.
Yet till we meet face to face
we can never be in synch,
our long distance voices like beggars
working the night.

Tropical Morning

Endless emoluments of green unfurl
an overbearing
moisture of scent where the lawn
relinquishes its clipped tribute
to civilization and plunges again
into a whorl of fragrance, colour, sound,
the burden of fertility. The damp
persuasiveness of death
pythons towards me. Fruits like indulgences
shudder and drop from low fronds bulbous with seed.
An upstart parakeet
comets across the mollified green air.
I am a new Adam lost for words.

Camping Trip

These few days each year
we live by the sun:
already at six
from tall trees nearby
phoebe and blackbird call,
light unstitches the canvas

My two sons still asleep,
I climb down to the shore;
the mountains opposite
solidify through haze.

The slow deliberate beat
of small waves against rock,
the silent wind in the pines—
all is unhurried routine.

The mind can resurface here,
slowly ideas will form
like water-boatmen skimming
over their own reflections.

Today like yesterday
we will do nothing, well—
explore a trail or swim,
gather shells, fish or read,

then, tired after supper, crawl
back to dark sleep again.
In the nearby campsites, fires,
voices across the lake.

In Muir Woods

Strange
        how we become
                silent
in the presence
        of tall trees
                almost
as if they were
        ancestors
                and we
granted an audience:
        in their leaves, needles,
                in their cool
distances we strain
        for messages, sealed
                in the bulwark
trunks, some breath
        of history, held
                some hope, an
aspiration.

Landscape Near Clifden

Fields full of gorse and rock, the wind
gusts fierce from the sea,
trees bend to the grey hills
past slate roofs jigged with smoke,
a few sheep in the yard,
stacks of cut turf.
Wool snags on the wire fence. I watch
as sea-birds whirr up like spray
from the rough shore
and hear the lark rise
through a black sky. It is all
stone wall, long grass, cold stream.
Now the mists start to fall
it is time to move on;
the ends of the earth are near.

Watershed

On my way up I think
'Now I'm above the tree-line, soon
it will all be different.'
Hesitant at times, the car's engine labours
like a human heart, seems liable to stall
before the final ascent.
But now I have made it;
calm in the sparse air,
I stroll around like a god
and look for rewards, some vast
regenerating vista. Brass tablets
on roadside boulders proclaim
this the Continental Divide,
elevation 12,000 feet;
I know from here on in
all rivers flow
westward to the Pacific.
But no endless panoramas:
though the weather is fine enough,
there's nothing to see except
further ranges, mesas and buttes,
no glint of the ultimate ocean.

Worth a photo anyway...
Then back in the car, buckled up,
I prepare for the many hairpins
still ahead before nightfall.

Preparations

In memory of Michael Thompson

At first he thinks it too much trouble, another journey.
Who needs it? And with no one expecting him!
His bones are brittle now, and his health poor.
There is so much to arrange: cancel the newspaper,
sort out the books and records,
find someone to feed the cats and tend the houseplants,
dispose of clothes, photograph albums,
shut off the water and gas, pull the curtains to.

No taxi has been summoned, no time set,
but, now it is done, all he can do is wait.
There are no addresses on the luggage labels.

Acknowledgements

Some of these poems have appeared, or will appear, in the following magazines and anthologies:

Akros (UK), Apostrophe (US), Ariel, Bywords, Canadian Forum, Confrontation (US), Contemporary Verse II, Dalhousie Review, The Fiddlehead, Literary Review of Canada, London Magazine (UK), Meanjin (Australia), Nashwaak Review, New Quarterly, Poetry Canada Review, Queens Quarterly, Takahe (New Zealand), Tickle Ace, Vintage 92, Wascana Review, Windhorse Review and Windsor Review.